*Spectacular*

# String-Pieced
# Quilts: A Pattern Book

**by the editors of *Traditional Quiltworks***
**and *Quilting Today* magazines**

CHITRA PUBLICATIONS

www.QuiltTownUSA.com

First printing: 2000
Library of Congress Cataloging-in-Publication Data

Spectacular string-pieced quilts : a pattern book / by the editors of Tradtional quiltworks and Quilting today.
        p. cm.
    ISBN 1-885588-36-4
    1. Patchwork--Patterns. 2. Patchwork quilts. I. Tradtional quiltworks. II. Quilting today.

TT835.S649 2001
746.46'041--dc21                                00-063880

Edited by Elsie M. Campbell, Debra Feece and Joyce Libal
Design & Illustration: Brenda Pytlik
Photography: VanZandbergen Photography, Brackney, PA and Stephen J. Appel, Vestal, NY

*Our Mission Statement:*
*We publish quality quilting magazines and books that recognize, promote and inspire self-expression. We are dedicated to serving our customers with respect, kindness and efficiency.*

# Dear Scrap Lovers,

What comes to mind when you hear the word "string"? Maybe you think of the ball of twine your mother used when she tied up packages or the string of pearls your great-aunt wore to church every Sunday. Perhaps you think of a much loved and now tattered string quilt your grandmother made for you.

Traditionally, string quilts are constructed from narrow strips of fabric left over after making clothing or other sewing projects. In string quilts, clashing prints become concerts of color as designs evolve spontaneously from a multitude of fabric scraps. The more fabrics the merrier when it comes to string quilts! String quilts are more about contrast and value than color coordination. The strings can gradate from light to dark across a block or they can be sewn in light/dark/light/dark stripe patterns. They can be sewn in parallel lines or at wild and wonderful angles. The freedom in design is marvelous.

There are two basic methods for constructing string-pieced blocks. The first involves sewing strips in a flip-and-sew style onto a foundation that can be paper, muslin or a lightweight nonfusible interfacing. If paper foundations are used, they are removed after the quilt top is constructed. Stitching on paper foundations and then removing them reduces the bulk in the finished quilt. This is especially important if you choose to quilt by hand. Muslin or interfacing foundations remain under the fabric scraps as an integral part of the quilt structure. This adds stability to the quilt along with warmth and weight.

The second method is to sew long strings of fabric together along their length until you have stitched a piece of fabric made up entirely of strings. Then blocks or pieces for blocks are cut from the fabricated yardage using a rotary cutter and ruler, or using traditional template methods as you would with any other yardage.

Both methods are described in detail in String-Piecing Instructions on page 4. You can choose to use either of these methods for many of the quilts in this book. When that is not the case, the pattern directions specify which method to use.

Now, dig out those bags, boxes and storage containers of scraps and get ready to experience the spontaneity of creating stunning quilts from strings!

*Piecefully yours,*

The Editors of
*Traditional Quiltworks*
magazine

*The editorial team, clockwise from the top, Jack Braunstein, Debra Feece, Deborah Hearn, Elsie Campbell and Joyce Libal*

# Contents

*The patterns are rated for difficulty. Look for these symbols with every pattern.*

Beginner     Intermediate     Advanced

# String-Piecing Instructions

Collect your fabric scraps and cut them into 1"- to 3"-wide strips. Select a pattern and read through the directions. You'll note that, for many of the patterns, you can choose either Option 1 or Option 2 to make the string-pieced sections of the quilt. Read through both options (described below) and decide which one you prefer.

## OPTION 1
### Foundation method:

This method makes string piecing accurate and easy to do. For each foundation, trace the foundation pattern onto paper, muslin or lightweight non-fusible interfacing, leaving a 1" space between foundations. Cut them out 1/2" beyond the traced lines. You will need one foundation for each block or portion of a block as indicated in the quilt pattern.

Cover the entire foundation with scraps of fabric in a random manner unless otherwise noted. Be generous with seam allowances when stitching scraps to a foundation because seam allowances less than 1/4" may pull out later and leave holes in the finished quilt. After stitching, trim the seam allowances to 1/4", if needed.

Some string-pieced blocks begin by centering a fabric scrap on the foundation. Fabric strips (strings) are then added to each side of the center fabric or in 'rounds' Log Cabin-style. Other blocks are made by working from one side or corner to the opposite side or corner, adding strings until the foundation is covered.

Begin by positioning a fabric scrap right side up on the foundation, as instructed in the pattern. NOTE: *If scraps are too short to cover an area of the foundation, join two or more scraps to make longer strings before stitching them to the foundation.* Hold the scrap in place with a pin or a dab of glue from a glue stick, if desired. Lay another scrap right side down on the first one, positioning it so that an edge of the first scrap is visible. This ensures that the first piece has the required seam allowance. Stitch at least 1/4" away from the raw edge of the uppermost fabric through both scraps and the foundation, as shown.

Trim the seam allowance of the scraps to 1/4" inch in one of the following ways:
• Use scissors being careful not to cut through the foundation.
• Fold the foundation out of your way along the stitching line. Cut the seam

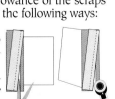

allowance using either scissors or a rotary cutter.

Turn the second scrap right side up, and press. Place a third scrap right-side down on the second scrap, stitch and trim, as before. Continue adding strings to the foundation in the same manner until the entire foundation is covered. NOTE: *If a foundation pattern contains a solid marked stitching line, trace that line on the wrong side of the foundation. Place fabric scraps on the right side of the foundation and turn the foundation wrong side up to stitch on the marked line.*

Baste each foundation in the seam allowance, halfway between the stitching line and the cutting line, to hold the fabric in place, if desired. Before assembling the quilt, trim the edges of the scrap strings even with the edge of the foundation.

Muslin or interfacing foundations become a permanent part of the quilt. Remove paper foundations before basting the quilt layers together. If the quilt has a border, do not remove paper foundations until the border has been added unless otherwise noted. Small bits of paper (1/4" pieces or smaller) can be left in the blocks. They will soften when laundering the quilt.

## OPTION 2
### String-pieced fabric method:

Using string-pieced fabric is an alternate method for making string-pieced blocks. Stitch two strings (strips of fabric) right sides together along their length. NOTE: *Use strings that are at least 22" long. Shorter strings can be sewn together end to end to make longer strings.*

Press the seam allowance toward one of the strings. Stitch a third string to a long side of the pieced strip in the same manner. Press the seam allowance in the same direction as before. Add more strings to the pieced panel until you have the amount indicated in the pattern. Cut pattern pieces from this yardage, using either plastic or freezer paper templates, as you would from any other fabric.

Since there are no foundations to provide stability for the outer edges of pieces in this method, you may wish to stabilize the string-pieced fabric with spray sizing or starch before cutting pattern pieces from it. NOTE: *Liquid starch is an inexpensive alternative to commercial spray sizing. Dilute the starch with equal amounts of water in a quart-sized plant mister bottle. Spray the string-pieced fabric and press it until completely dry.*

## TEMPLATES
### Plastic templates:

Place a sheet of firm, clear plastic over the patterns and trace the cutting line and/or stitching line for each one. Templates for machine piecing include seam allowances; templates for hand piecing generally do not. Use a permanent marker to record the name and size of the block, the grainline and the number of pieces needed to complete one block on every template.

In most cases, patterns for templates are full-size. If only half of a pattern is provided, trace it onto paper. Then fold the paper along the line indicated on the pattern. Unfold the paper and align the fold with the line indicated on the pattern. Trace the second half of the pattern. Use this paper pattern to make your template.

Trace around the template on the string-pieced fabric in the same manner as for other fabric.

### Tracing templates:

Test marking tools for removability before using them. Sharpen pencils often. Align the grainline on the template with the grainline of the fabric. Place a piece of fine sandpaper beneath the fabric to prevent slipping, if desired. For machine piecing, mark the right side. For hand piecing, mark the wrong side of the fabric unless otherwise noted, and flip all directional (asymmetrical) templates before tracing them. Mark and cut just enough pieces to make a sample block. Piece the block to be sure your templates are accurate. Handle bias edges carefully to avoid stretching.

### Freezer paper templates:

As an alternative to making plastic templates, you may wish to make templates from freezer paper. This saves time because you do not need to trace around the template for each piece.

Place a piece of freezer paper, shiny side down, over the patterns and trace the cutting line for each one. Make one template for every 10 to 12 fabric pieces. Cut the templates out. With a dry iron set on cotton, adhere the freezer paper templates, shiny side down, to the right side of the string-pieced fabric. Cut out the fabric pieces along the edge of the freezer paper templates. Use scissors to cut curved pieces. Use a rotary cutter and ruler for straight edges.

Remove the freezer paper templates and reuse them. They will usually adhere to fabric up to a dozen times.

# General Directions

Read through the directions in the pattern before cutting fabric for any of the projects. String-pieced yardage requirements listed under Option 2 are based on 22"-wide fabric, unless noted otherwise in the pattern. Yardage is based on 44"-wide fabric with a useable width of 42". Pattern pieces are full-size and include a 1/4" seam allowance as do all dimensions given. An "R" means the piece must be reversed before tracing. We recommend making a sample block before cutting fabric for the entire quilt.

## FABRICS

We suggest using 100% cotton. Wash fabric in warm water with mild detergent. Do not use fabric softener. Wash darks separately and check for bleeding during the rinse cycle. Since string quilts are made from a variety of fabrics—both light and dark—this step is extremely important. Eliminate any fabrics that bleed because bleeding is likely to continue each time the quilt is laundered. You may find it helpful to sort the fabric by value—light, medium and dark—before you begin piecing.

## CUTTING

All dimensions given in the patterns include a 1/4" seam allowance. Cut lengthwise strips for borders parallel to the selvage before cutting other pieces from that yardage.

Strings are narrow strips of fabric that are left over from other sewing projects. If you do not have strips of scrap fabric, new yardage can be cut into strings (1"- to 3"-wide strings work best). Cut any scraps that are wider than 3" into narrower strings.

## PRESSING

Press with a dry iron. As you join pieces for the quilt top, press seam allowances toward the darker of the two pieces whenever possible. Otherwise, trim away 1/16" from the darker seam allowance to prevent it from showing through. Press all blocks, sashings and borders before assembling the quilt top.

## MITERED BORDERS

Measure the length of the quilt top and add 2 times the border width plus 2" to that number. Cut border strips this measurement. Match the center of the quilt top with the center of the border strip and pin to the corners. Stitch; beginning, ending and backstitching each seamline 1/4" from the edge of the quilt top. After all borders have been attached, miter one corner at a time. With the quilt top right side down, lay one border over the other. Draw a

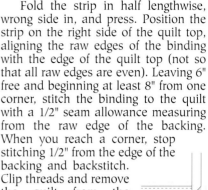

straight line at a 45° angle from the inner to the outer corner.

Reverse the positions of the borders and mark another corner-to-corner line. With the borders right sides together and the marked seamlines carefully matched, stitch from the inner to the outer corner, backstitching at the inner corner. Open the mitered seam to make sure it lies flat, then trim the excess fabric 1/4" beyond the stitching line and press.

## FINISHING YOUR QUILT

### Marking Quilting Lines

Mark before basting the quilt together with the batting and backing. Chalk pencils show well on dark fabrics; otherwise use a very hard (#3 or #4) pencil or other marker for this purpose. Test your marker first. Transfer paper designs by placing fabric over the design and tracing. A light box may be necessary for darker fabrics. Precut plastic stencils that fit the area you wish to quilt may be placed on top of the quilt and traced. Use a ruler to mark straight, even grids.

Outline quilting does not require marking. Simply eyeball 1/4" from the seam or stitch "in the ditch" (next to the seam).

Masking tape can also be used to mark straight lines. Temporary quilting stencils can be made from clear adhesive-backed paper or freezer paper and reused many times. To avoid residue, do not leave tape or adhesive-backed paper on your quilt overnight.

### BASTING

Cut the batting and backing at least 2" larger than the quilt top on all sides. Tape the backing, wrong side up, on a flat surface to anchor it. Smooth the batting on top, followed by the quilt top, right side up. Baste the three layers together to form a quilt sandwich. Begin at the center and baste horizontally, then vertically. Place lines of basting no more than 6" apart.

### BINDING

After quilting either by hand or by machine, trim excess batting and backing even to within 1/4" of the quilt top. Cut binding strips with the grain for straight-edge quilts. To make 1/2" finished binding, cut 2 1/2" wide strips. Sew the strips together with diagonal seams; trim the seam allowances and press seams open.

Fold the strip in half lengthwise, wrong side in, and press. Position the strip on the right side of the quilt top, aligning the raw edges of the binding with the edge of the quilt top (not so that all raw edges are even). Leaving 6" free and beginning at least 8" from one corner, stitch the binding to the quilt with a 1/2" seam allowance measuring from the raw edge of the backing. When you reach a corner, stop stitching 1/2" from the edge of the backing and backstitch. Clip threads and remove the quilt from the machine. Fold the binding up and away from the quilt, forming a 45° angle, as shown. Keeping the angled fold secure, fold the binding back down. This fold should be even with the edge of the quilt top. Begin stitching at the fold through all the layers.

Continue stitching around the quilt in this manner to within 6" of the starting point. To finish, fold both strips back along the edge of the quilt so that the folded edges meet about 3" from both lines of stitching and the binding lies flat on the quilt. Finger press to crease the folds. Cut both strips 1 1/4" from the folds.

Open both strips and place the ends at right angles to each other, right sides together. Fold the bulk of the quilt out of your way. Join the strips with a diagonal seam, as shown.

Trim the seam allowance to 1/4" and press it open. Refold the joined strip wrong side in. Place the binding flat against the quilt and finish stitching it to the quilt. Trim the edge of the layers as needed so that the binding edge will be filled with batting as you fold the binding to the back of the quilt.

Blindstitch the binding to the back of the quilt, covering the seamline.

Remove visible markings. Sign and date your quilt.

# 1940's Quilt

*Solid stars and bright sashing bring harmony to scrappy blocks.*

**QUILT SIZE:** 69" x 85"
**BLOCK SIZE:** 12" square

## MATERIALS
***Use Option 1 to make this quilt.***
*(Refer to* String-Piecing Instructions.*)*

• Assorted prints and solids, totaling at least 2 1/2 yards
• 20 fat eighths (11" x 18") assorted solids
• 3 yards green print
• 3/4 yard light print for the binding
• 5 yards backing fabric
• 73" x 89" piece of batting
• Paper, muslin or lightweight non-fusible interfacing for the foundations

## CUTTING
***For each of 20 blocks:***
• Cut 4: 4" x 7" rectangles, one solid, for the star points
*Also:*
• Cut 5: 4 1/2" x 80" lengthwise strips, green print, for the vertical sashings
• Cut 2: 4 1/2" x 72" lengthwise strips, green print, for the border
• Cut 16: 4 1/2" x 12 1/2" strips, green print, for the horizontal sashings
• Cut 8: 2 1/2" x 44" strips, light print, for the binding

## DIRECTIONS
*Refer to* String-Piecing Instructions *to make the full-size pattern template and to piece the foundations.*
• Trace the full-size pattern 80 times on the foundation material, leaving a 1" space between foundations. Cut each one out 1/2" beyond the traced lines. Draw the marked star point stitching lines on each foundation.
***For each of 20 blocks:***
• Position a 4" x 7" solid rectangle, right side up, to cover the star point in the center of a foundation.
• Lay a scrap string right side down on one long side of the solid rectangle, positioning one long edge 1/4" beyond the drawn stitching line on the foundation. Stitch them together along the drawn stitching line, as shown.

• Trim the seam allowance to 1/4". Fold the string right side up and press.
• In the same manner, lay a scrap string right side down on the opposite side of the solid rectangle and stitch.
• Continue adding strings until the foundation is covered, to make a quarter block. Make 4, using the same solid for the star points.
• Trim the foundations on the drawn lines.
• Lay 2 quarter blocks right sides together matching star points. Stitch them together along a short side to make a half block, as shown. Make 2.

• Stitch the 2 half-blocks together, to complete a block.

## ASSEMBLY
• Lay out 5 blocks alternately with four 4 1/2" x 12 1/2" green print strips in a vertical row. Stitch them together. Make 4.
• Measure the length of a row. Trim the five 4 1/2" x 80" green print strips to that measurement to make vertical sashing strips.
• Referring to the quilt photo, lay out the rows alternately with the five trimmed vertical sashing strips. Join the rows and sashing strips.
• Measure the width of the quilt. Trim the 4 1/2" x 72" strips to that measurement and stitch them to the remaining sides of the quilt.
• If you used paper foundations, remove them now.
• Finish the quilt as described in the *General Directions,* using the 2 1/2" x 44" light print strips for the binding.

*(The pattern piece for "1940's Quilt" is on page 31.)*

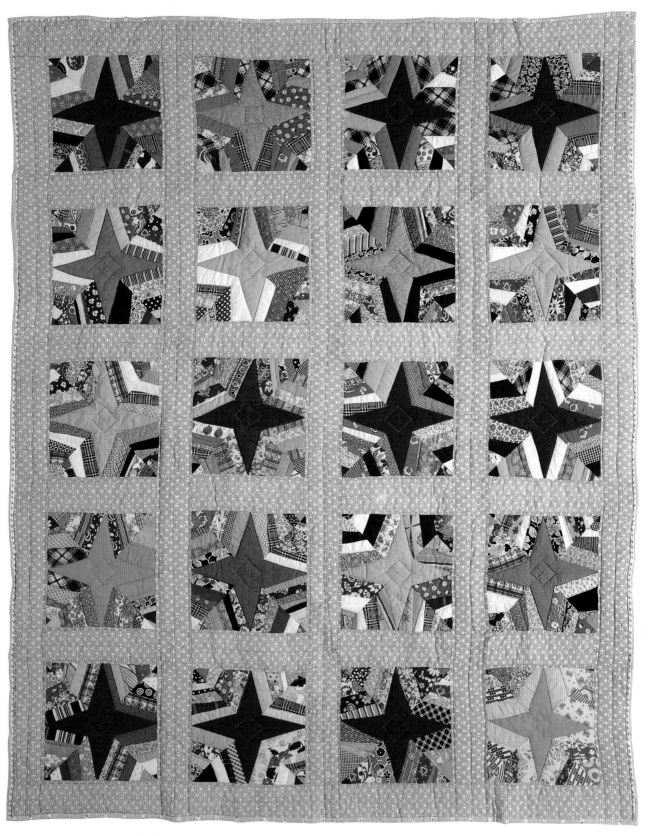

*Julia Gladys Mitchell Lancaster pieced **"1940's Quilt"** (69" x 85") prior to her untimely death in 1943. More than 50 years had elapsed when her son Johnny Lancaster gave the top to Violette Harris Denney of Carrollton, Georgia. Violette backed the top with feedsack fabrics from her own mother's stash and then hand quilted it.*

# String Star

by Linda Pool

 *Use scraps cleverly in this traditional quilt.*

**QUILT SIZE:** 41 1/2" x 52"
**BLOCK SIZE:** 5 1/2" square

## MATERIALS

***Use option 1 to make this quilt.*** *(Refer to String-Piecing Instructions.)*

• Assorted prints and solids totaling at least 3 yards
• 2 yards navy print for the blocks, outer border and binding
• 1/2 yard muslin
• 1 1/2 yards backing fabric
• 46" x 56" piece of batting
• Paper, muslin or lightweight non-fusible interfacing for the foundations

## CUTTING

• Cut 2: 3" x 44" lengthwise strips, navy print, for the outer border
• Cut 2: 3" x 56" lengthwise strips, navy print, for the outer border
• Cut 5: 2 1/2" x 44" strips, navy print, for the binding
• Cut 220: B, navy print
• Cut 24: C, muslin, for the inner border
• Cut 4 each: D and DR, muslin
• Cut 5: 1" x 44" strips, muslin, then cut one in half to yield two 1" x 22" strips, for the middle border

## DIRECTIONS

*Refer to* String-Piecing Instructions *to piece the foundations.*
• Trace the A pattern 192 times on the foundation material, leaving a 1" space between foundations. Cut each one out 1/2" beyond the traced lines. Draw the marked solid stitching line on each foundation.
• Starting at the wide end of a foundation, stitch one print or solid fabric scrap in position 1 and random width strips of assorted prints and solids to cover the remainder of the foundation. NOTE: *To create squares at the junctions of the blocks when they are joined together, use the same or coordinating print or solid scraps in the first position of each of 4 foundations.*
• Trim the foundations on the drawn lines. Make 192.
• Stitch a string-pieced A to a navy print B, as shown, to make a pieced unit. Make 192. Set 4 aside for the corner blocks.

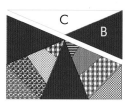

## ASSEMBLY

• Referring to the quilt photo and Assembly Diagram on page 9, lay out the pieced units in 16 rows of 12. Match or coordinate fabrics to form squares at the junctions of the blocks.
• Starting at the upper left corner of the layout, sew a D to the first pieced unit. Stitch a navy print B to a DR and join the units, as shown to make a corner unit. Return it to the layout.

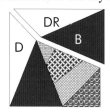

• Sew the next 2 pieced units together. Sew a navy B to a muslin C and join the units, as shown, to make an edge unit. Return it to the layout.

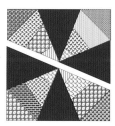

• Continue across the top row, making 4 more edge units and one more corner unit.
• Starting at the beginning of the next row, make an edge unit, as before. Return it to the layout.
• Sew the next 4 pieced units into pairs and join the pairs, as shown, to make a block.

• Continue across the row, making 4 more blocks and an edge unit.
• Assemble the remaining units in rows. Join the rows.

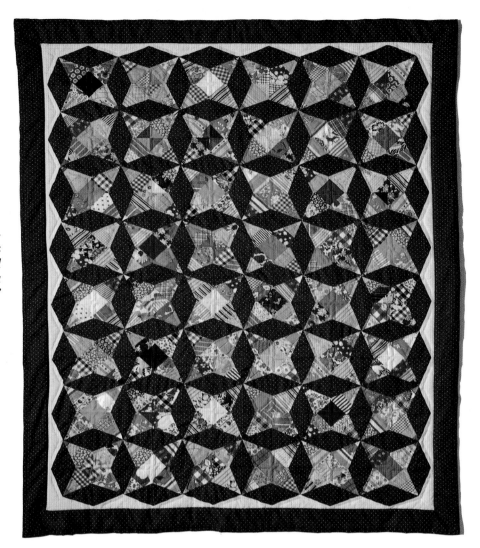

Linda Pool of Vienna, Virginia, cleverly recut an anonymous quilter's blocks to create this country-flavored **"String Star"** *(41 1/2" x 52")*. *"It's a great way to use all kinds of scraps!" Linda notes.*

**Assembly Diagram**

**For the borders:**

• Stitch a 1" x 44" muslin strip to a 3" x 44" navy print strip, right sides together along their length, to make a short pieced border. Make 2.

• Center and stitch the short pieced borders to the short sides of the quilt, keeping the muslin against the quilt. Start, stop and backstitch 1/4" from each edge.

• Stitch a 1" x 22" muslin strip to a 1" x 44" muslin strip, end to end, to make a long muslin strip. Make 2.

• Center and stitch a long muslin strip and a 3" x 56" navy print strip, right sides together along their length, to make a long pieced border. Make 2.

• Center and stitch the long pieced border to the remaining sides of the quilt. Start, stop and backstitch 1/4" from each edge, as before.

• Miter the corners according to the *General Directions.*

• Finish the quilt as described in the *General Directions*, using the 2 1/2" x 44" navy print strips for the binding.

*(The pattern pieces for "String Star" are on page 30.)*

9

# String-Pieced Snowball

*See what you can do with yellow!*

**QUILT SIZE:** 49" x 89"

## MATERIALS
***Choose either Option 1 or Option 2 to make this quilt.*** *(Refer to* String-Piecing Instructions.*)*

*For Option 1:*
• Assorted prints and solids, totaling at least 2 1/2 yards
• Paper, muslin or lightweight non-fusible interfacing for the foundations
*For Option 2:*
• 7 1/2 yards of 22"-wide string pieced fabric. (*Refer to* String-Piecing Instructions.)
• Freezer paper or template plastic
*Also:*
• 2 1/2 yards yellow solid

• 1/2 yard yellow print, for the binding
• 4 1/2 yards backing fabric
• 53" x 93" piece of batting
• Template plastic or freezer paper

## CUTTING
• Cut 150: B, yellow solid
• Cut 7: 2 1/2" x 44" strips, yellow print, for the binding

## DIRECTIONS
*Option 1:*
*Follow the* String-Piecing Instructions *to piece the foundations.*
• Trace the A pattern 264 times on the foundation material, leaving a 1" space between foundations. Cut each one out 1/2" beyond the traced lines.

• Beginning in the center of an A foundation, and working in both directions toward the ends, sew random width strips of assorted prints and solids on the foundation until it is covered, as shown.
• Trim the foundation on the drawn lines. Make 264.

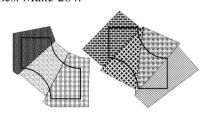

• Mark dots on the wrong side of each foundation as indicated on the pattern.

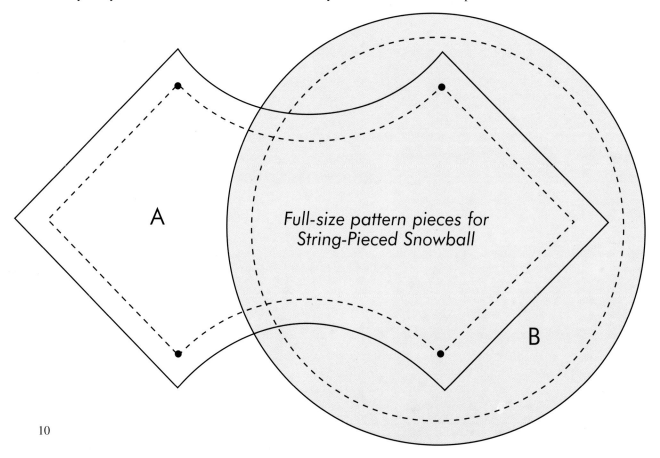

A

*Full-size pattern pieces for String-Pieced Snowball*

B

### Option 2:

• Use either template plastic or freezer paper and directions in *String-Piecing Instructions* to cut 264 A's from string-pieced fabric.

### For the snowball blocks:

• Stitch 2 A's together to make a half-circle, as shown. Make 132.

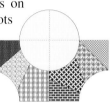

• If you used paper foundations, gently remove them now.

NOTE: *The construction of the remainder of this quilt is a good candidate for traditional hand piecing.*

• Fold a yellow B in half and then in quarters. Crease the folds.

• Unfold the yellow B and align a crease with the center seam of a half-circle, right sides together, and pin it in place. Align the creases on each side of that crease with the dots on the A pieces and pin, as before. Stitch the B to the half-circle, backstitching at the dot on each A piece to make a snowball unit. Make 66.

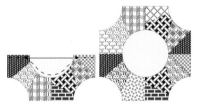

• Stitch a remaining half-circle to the snowball unit, matching creases to seams, as before. Fold the unit in half, right side in, and align the unstitched edges of the adjacent A pieces. Stitch them together from outer edges to the dots, backstitching at the dots to complete a Snowball block. Make 66.

• Stitch 6 Snowball blocks together to form a row, as shown. Make 11.

• Stitch 7 yellow B's along the lower edge of each snowball row, as shown.

• Stitch the remaining yellow B's along the upper edge of one snowball row to make a top row, as shown.

*"String-Pieced Snowball"* (49" x 89") is a stunning example of the old quilt tops Patricia DePoyster of Claremont, New Hampshire, purchases and then completes. Make your own version, using either modern fabrics or reproduction prints that closely match the original quilt.

### ASSEMBLY

• Beginning with the top row, lay out the 11 rows so that the yellow B's fill in the arcs in the preceding row, referring to the quilt photo as needed. Join the rows.

• Trim the yellow B's along the outer edges, even with the edges of the A's as show.

• Finish the quilt as described in the *General Directions*, using the 2 1/2" x 44" yellow print strips for the binding.

# Eight Point Stars

 *String Stars span the centuries when made with lots of old-time scraps!*

**QUILT SIZE:** 78" square
**BLOCK SIZE:** 15 3/8" square

## MATERIALS

***Choose either Option 1 or Option 2 to make this quilt.** (Refer to* String-Piecing Instructions.*)*

***For Option 1:***
• Assorted prints and solids, totaling at least 3 5/8 yards
• Paper, muslin or lightweight non-fusible interfacing for the foundations
***For Option 2:***
• 6 1/2 yards of 22"-wide string-pieced fabric *(Refer to* String-Piecing Instructions.*)*
• Freezer paper or template plastic
***Also:***
• 3 1/2 yards muslin
• 3/4 yard navy pin-dot for the binding
• 4 3/4 yards backing fabric
• 82" square piece of batting

## CUTTING
• Cut 100: 5 1/2" squares, muslin
• Cut 25: 8" squares, muslin, then cut them in quarters diagonally to yield 100 triangles
• Cut 8: 2 1/2" x 44" strips, navy pin-dot, for the binding

## DIRECTIONS
***Option 1:***
*Follow the* String-Piecing Instructions *to make the full-size pattern template and piece the foundations.*
• Trace the full-size pattern 200 times on the foundation material, leaving a 1" space between foundations. Cut each one out 1/2" beyond the traced lines.
• Stitch random width strips of assorted prints and solids to each foundation until it is covered, as shown, to make a star point.

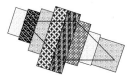

• Trim the foundation on the drawn lines. Make 200.
• Mark dots on the wrong side of each foundation as indicated on the pattern.
***Option 2:***
• Use either template plastic or freezer paper and directions in *String-Piecing Instructions* to cut 200 string-pieced star points from string-pieced fabric.
***For each of 25 blocks:***
• Place 2 star points right sides together and sew between the dots, as shown, backstitching at each dot.

• Set in a 5 1/2" muslin square to make a quarter-star. Make 4. NOTE: *The muslin squares and triangles are slightly oversized to allow for squar-*

*ing the completed blocks.*
• Join 2 quarter-stars, stitching between the dots, as before, to make a half-star. Make 2.

• Join the half-stars, matching the center seams and backstitching at the outer dots. Set a muslin triangle into each side to complete a block.

• If you used paper for the foundations, gently remove them now.
• Trim each block 1/4" beyond the tips of the star points.
• Lay out the blocks in 5 rows of 5. Stitch the blocks into rows and join the rows.
• Finish the quilt as described in the *General Directions,* using the 2 1/2" x 44" navy pin-dot strips for the binding.

When Lila Lee Jones of Drexel, Missouri, purchased the 19th century blocks for *"Eight Point Stars"* (78" square), they were set with more-recent blue stripe fabric squares and triangles. She and her friends spent hours picking out the tiny machine stitches to remove the inappropriate background fabric. Lila chose to replace the background with muslin that doesn't compete with the antique fabrics of the stars.

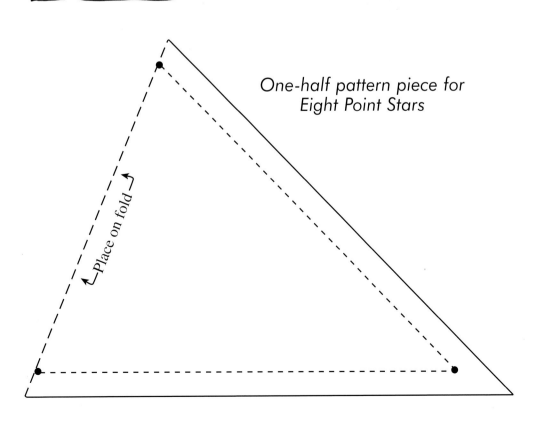

One-half pattern piece for *Eight Point Stars*

Place on fold

# Diamond Strings with Lattice

*Muslin latticework polishes these diamonds-in-the-rough.*

**QUILT SIZE:** 77 1/2" x 79 1/2"

## MATERIALS

***Choose either Option 1 or Option 2 to make this quilt.** (Refer to* String-Piecing Instructions.*)*

***For Option 1:***
- Assorted prints and solids, totaling at least 6 1/4 yards
- Paper, muslin or lightweight non-fusible interfacing for the foundations

***For Option 2:***
- 8 1/2 yards of 22"-wide string-pieced fabric *(Refer to* String-Piecing Instructions.*)*
- Freezer paper or template plastic

***Also:***
- 3 1/4 yards muslin
- 2 1/2 yards print for the border
- 3/4 yard green for the binding
- 4 3/4 yards backing fabric
- 82" x 84" piece of batting

## CUTTING
- Cut 5: 2" x 108" lengthwise strips, muslin, for the lattice
- Cut 2: 2" x 78" lengthwise strips, muslin, for the lattice
- Cut 2: 2" x 66" lengthwise strips, muslin, for the lattice
- Cut 2: 2" x 42" lengthwise strips, muslin, for the lattice
- Cut 2: 2" x 30" lengthwise strips, muslin, for the lattice
- Cut 2: 2" x 10" strips, muslin, for the lattice
- Cut 108: B, muslin

- Cut 4: 2 1/4" x 80" strips, print, for the border
- Cut 8: 2 1/2" x 44" strips, green, for the binding

## DIRECTIONS
### Option 1:
*Follow the* String-Piecing Instructions *to piece the foundations.*
- Trace the A pattern 124 times on the foundation material, leaving a 1" space between foundations. Cut each one out 1/2" beyond the traced lines.
- Beginning in the center of a foundation, stitch random width strips of assorted prints and solids to it until it is covered, as shown.

- Trim the foundation on the drawn lines. Make 124.
### Option 2:
- Use either template plastic or freezer paper and directions in *String-Piecing Instructions* to cut 124 A's from string-pieced fabric.

## ASSEMBLY
- Referring to the Assembly Diagram, lay out the A's alternately with the muslin B's in diagonal rows. Lay out the 2"-wide muslin lattice strips between the rows, making sure that the longest ones are toward the center.
- Stitch the string-pieced A's and

muslin B's into diagonal rows.
- Stitch a diagonal row with 13 A's to a 2" x 108" muslin lattice strip, as shown.
- Align a ruler with one edge of a diamond. With a fabric marker or pencil, make marks in the seam allowance of the lattice strip, as shown. Make the marks in line with the muslin B's. Use these marks to align the next row.

- Stitch an adjacent diamond row to the lattice strip, carefully matching the seams to the marks, to make a diamond panel.
- Continue adding diamond rows and lattice strips alternately until all rows are joined.
- Trim the outer edges of the quilt 1/4" beyond the center point of the outer diamonds, as shown.
- Measure the length of the quilt. Trim 2 of the 2 1/4" x 80" print border strips to that measurement and stitch them to the long sides of the quilt.

*Pat DePoyster of Claremont, New Hampshire, makes a habit of rescuing antique quilt tops and turning them into unique quilts. She finished this unusual diagonally-sashed **"Diamond Strings with Lattice"** (77 1/2" x 79 1/2") with all-over machine quilting.*

**Assembly Diagram**

• Measure the width of the quilt, including the borders. Trim the remaining 2 1/4" x 80" print strips to that measurement and stitch them to the remaining sides of the quilt.
• If you used paper foundations, remove them now.
• Finish the quilt as described in the *General Directions,* using the 2 1/2" x 44" green strips for the binding.

*(The pattern pieces for "Diamond Strings with Lattice" are on page 32.)*

# Too Much Pink

 *Turn one block in an unexpected direction to 'shake things up'!*

**QUILT SIZE**: 46" x 54"
**BLOCK SIZE:** 4" square

## MATERIALS
***Choose either Option 1 or Option 2 to make this quilt.** (Refer to String-Piecing Instructions.)*

***For Option 1:***
• Assorted solids totaling at least 2 1/2 yards
• Paper, muslin or lightweight non-fusible interfacing for the foundations
***For Option 2:***
• 20 fat eighths (11" x 18") assorted solids
***Also:***
• 2 1/4 yards black
• 3 yards backing fabric
• 50" x 58" piece of batting
• Template plastic

## CUTTING
***For Option 1:***
• Cut 34: 5 1/2" squares, foundation material, then cut them in half to yield 68 triangle foundations. You will use 67.
***For Option 2:***
• Cut 102: 18"-long strips of various widths from 1" to 1 1/4", assorted solids
***Also:***
• Cut 60: 18"-long strips of various widths from 1" to 1 1/4", assorted solids
• Cut 4: 3 1/2" x 50" lengthwise strips, black for the outer border
• Cut 5: 2 1/2" x 50" lengthwise strips, black for the binding
• Cut 4: 3" x 40" lengthwise strips, black for the inner border
• Cut 34: 5 1/2" squares, black, then cut them in half diagonally to yield 68

triangles. You will use 67.

## DIRECTIONS
***Option 1:***
*Follow the* String-Piecing Instructions *to piece the foundations.*
• Beginning at the base of a triangle foundation, stitch random width assorted solid strips to it until it is covered, as shown.

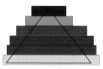

• Trim the edges of the strips even with the edge of the foundation. Make 67.

***Option 2:***
• Stitch random width 18"-long strips together, along their length, to form a 3 1/2"-wide pieced panel. Make 17.
• Using template A, mark and cut 4 pieced triangles from each of the pieced panels, for a total of 68. You will use 67.

## ASSEMBLY
• Stitch a black triangle to a pieced triangle, right sides together, to make a Sunshine & Shadows block, as shown. Make 67. Set 4 aside for the border.

• Trim each of the remaining 63 blocks to 4 1/2" square, being careful to

keep the diagonal seamline between the black and strip-pieced triangles centered.
• Referring to the quilt photo as needed, lay out 63 blocks in 9 rows of 7. Stitch them into rows and join the rows.
• Measure the length of the quilt. Trim two 3" x 40" black strips to that measurement. Sew them to the long sides of the quilt.
• Measure the width of the quilt, including the borders. Trim the remaining 3" x 40" black strips to that measurement. Sew them to the remaining sides of the quilt.
***For the pieced borders:***
• Stitch random width 18"-long strips together, along their length, to form a 3 1/2"-wide pieced panel. Make 10.
• Cut five 3 1/2" slices from each pieced panel, for a total of 50.

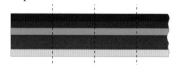

• Stitch 14 slices together, as shown, to make a long border. Make 2.

• Stitch them to the long sides of the quilt. Remove one or 2 of the fabric strips as necessary to fit the quilt.
• In the same manner, join 11 slices to make a short border. Make 2.
• Trim the 4 remaining Sunshine & Shadows blocks to 3 1/2" square being careful to keep the diagonal seam-line between the black and strip-pieced trian-gles centered.

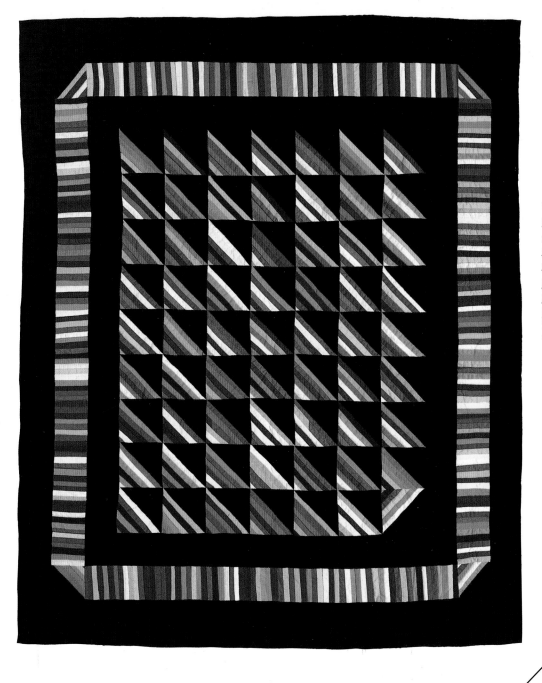

*Virginia Jones of Taunton, Massachusetts, found refuge in making this high-contrast, solid-color string quilt. She'd spent long stretches of time piecing an overwhelmingly pastel quilt for a pink-loving friend and needed a break! This quilt was her answer to* **"Too Much Pink"** *(46" x 54")!*

• Stitch a trimmed block to each short end of the short borders, as shown.

• Stitch the short borders to the remaining sides of the quilt.
• Trim two 3 1/2" x 50" black strips to fit the quilt's length. Sew them to the long sides of the quilt.
• Trim the remaining 3 1/2" x 50" black strips to fit the quilt's width and sew them to the remaining sides of the quilt.

• Finish the quilt as described in the *General Directions,* using the 2 1/2" x 50" black strips for the binding.

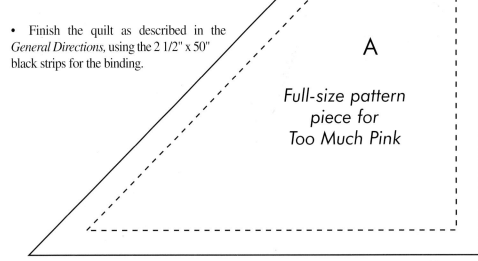

A

*Full-size pattern piece for Too Much Pink*

# Alex's Crazy Vacation Quilt

*Make a contemporary-looking quilt with traditional string-piecing.*

**QUILT SIZE:** 44 3/4" x 63"
**BLOCK SIZE:** 6 1/2" square

## MATERIALS

*Use Option 1 to make this quilt:*
*(Refer to* String-Piecing Instructions.*)*

• Assorted prints and solids totaling at least 1 1/2 yards
• 2 yards mottled blue print
• 1/2 yard red for the binding
• 3 3/4 yards backing fabric
• 49" x 67" piece of batting
• Paper, muslin or lightweight non-fusible interfacing for the foundations

## CUTTING

• Cut 2: 4" x 58" lengthwise strips, blue print, for the border
• Cut 2: 4" x 48" lengthwise strips, blue print, for the border
• Cut 15: 7" squares, blue print
• Cut 2: 5 1/2" squares, blue print, then cut them in half diagonally to yield 4 corner triangles
• Cut 4: 10 1/2" squares, blue print, then cut them in quarters diagonally to yield 16 setting triangles
• Cut 6: 2 1/2" x 44" strips, red, for the binding
• Cut 24: 8" squares, foundation material

## DIRECTIONS

**Option 1:**
*Follow the* String-Piecing Instructions *to piece the foundations.*

• The 8" square foundations are randomly pieced. For some blocks, place a bright print or solid scrap roughly in the center of a foundation, right side up, as shown.

• Stitch assorted scraps to the foundation working around the center scrap, until the foundation is covered.
• For other blocks, stitch random width assorted print and sold strips to the foundation, as desired. Make 24 blocks.

• Trim the foundations to 7" square.

## ASSEMBLY

• Referring to the Assembly Diagram, lay out the blocks, 7" blue print squares, setting triangles and corner triangles, as shown.
• Stitch them into diagonal rows and join the rows.
• Measure the length of the quilt. Trim the 4" x 58" blue print strips to that measurement and stitch them to the long sides of the quilt.

• Measure the width of the quilt, including the borders. Trim the 4" x 48" blue print strips to that measurement and stitch them to the remaining sides of the quilt.
• If you used paper foundations, remove them now.
• Finish the quilt as described in the *General Directions,* using the 2 1/2" x 44" red strips for the binding.

**Assembly Diagram**

*Eleven year-old Alex Ford of Yuma, Arizona, made **"Alex's Crazy Vacation Quilt"** (44 3/4" x 63") with scraps from his favorite aunt's fabric stash. He used school vacations while in the sixth grade to complete the quilt. Constructed as a 4-H project, Alex's quilt won 2 ribbons at his county fair.*

# String Scrap

*Use odds and ends to make a colorful quilt in record time!*

**QUILT SIZE:** 72 1/2" x 91 1/2"
**BLOCK SIZE:** 9 1/2" square

## MATERIALS
***Use Option 1 to make this quilt.** (Refer to* String-Piecing Instructions.*)*

• Assorted print scraps, totaling at least 6 1/2 yards
• Paper, muslin or lightweight non-fusible interfacing for the foundations
***Also:***
• 2 3/4 yards gray print
• 5 1/2 yards backing fabric
• 77" x 96" piece of batting

## CUTTING
• Cut 4: 2 1/2" x 90" lengthwise strips, gray print, for the binding
• Cut 2: 3" x 88" lengthwise strips, gray print, for the side borders
• Cut 2: 3" x 75" lengthwise strips, gray print, for the top and bottom borders
NOTE: *The quiltmaker chose to make the top and bottom borders narrower than the sides. If you want to do the same, cut the 75" gray print strips 1 3/4"-wide.*
• Cut 63: 1 7/8" x 15" strips, gray print
• Cut 63: 11" squares, foundation material

## DIRECTIONS
*Follow the* String-Piecing Instructions *to piece the foundations.*
• Center a 1 7/8" x 15" gray print strip diagonally, right side up, on a foundation.

• Stitch random width assorted print strips to the left and right sides of the gray strip until the foundation is covered.
• Trim the foundations to 10" square. Make 63.

## ASSEMBLY
• Referring to the quilt photo, lay out the blocks in 9 rows of 7, alternating the direction of the strings in each block.
• Stitch the blocks into rows and join the rows.
• Measure the length of the quilt. Trim the 3" x 88" gray print strips to that measurement. Stitch them to the long sides of the quilt.
• Measure the width of the quilt, including the borders. Trim the 3" x 75" strips to that measurement. Stitch them to the remaining sides of the quilt.
• Finish the quilt as described in the *General Directions,* using the 2 1/2" x 90" gray print strips for the binding.

*Margaret Gray of Ottawa, Kansas, used plenty of her scraps in **"String Scrap"** (72 1/2" x 91 1/2"). Each block features a subtle gray print strip that runs through the center providing continuity and the effect of diagonal sashing strips with blocks turned on point.*

# Scrap Happy

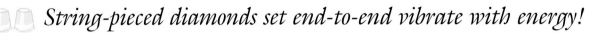 *String-pieced diamonds set end-to-end vibrate with energy!*

**QUILT SIZE:** 71" x 81"

## MATERIALS
***Choose either Option 1 or Option 2
to make this quilt.*** *(Refer to* String-
Piecing Instructions.*)*

***For Option 1:***
• Assorted prints and solids totaling
at least 5 yards
• Paper, muslin or lightweight non-
fusible interfacing for the foundations
***For Option 2:***
• 7 1/2 yards of 36"-wide string-
pieced fabric *(Refer to* String-Piecing
Instructions.*)*
• Freezer Paper
***Also:***
• 7/8 yard print for the binding
• 5 1/2 yards backing fabric
• 75" x 95" piece of batting

## CUTTING
***Option 1:***
• Cut 9: 10 1/2" x 75" lengthwise
strips, foundation material
• Cut 4: 16" squares, foundation
material
***Option 2:***
• Cut 1: 10 1/2" x 75" lengthwise
strip, freezer paper
• Cut 1: 16" square, freezer paper
***Also:***
• Cut 8: 2 1/2" x 44" strips, print,
for the binding

## PREPARATION
• Place a ruler on one end of a
10 1/2" x 75" strip of foundation material for Option 1; or a strip of freezer

paper for Option 2. Make a 45° angle
cut, as shown.

• Mark a point 14 3/4" from the first
cut at both the top and bottom edges
of the foundation or freezer paper
strip. With a fabric marker or pencil,
draw a straight line between the
marks. Measure the smaller angle. It
should be 45°. Adjust the line, if necessary, to achieve a 45° angle and cut
along the marked line to make a diamond foundation for Option 1 or a
diamond template for Option 2.

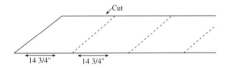

## DIRECTIONS
***Option 1:***
*Follow the* String-Piecing Instructions
*to piece the foundations.*
• Make 35 foundations as described
above.
• Beginning in the center of a foundation diamond, stitch random width
strips of assorted prints and solids to
the left and right sides until the foundation is covered, as shown.

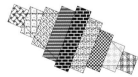

• Trim the edges of the strips even
with the edge of the foundation. Make 35.

• In the same manner, position a
random width strip diagonally across
the center of a 16" foundation square.
Stitch random width strips to the left
and right sides to cover the square.
Trim the edges of the strips even with
the edge of the foundation. Make 4.
***Option 2:***
• Use diamond freezer paper templates and directions in *String-Piecing
Instructions*, to make 35 diamonds
from string-pieced fabric. Position the
templates on the fabric as shown. Cut
out the pieces along the outer edge of
the freezer paper templates.

• Position the 16" square freezer
paper template on the string-pieced
fabric, as shown.

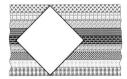

• In the same manner as for the diamonds, adhere the template and cut
out the square. Make 4.

*Patricia DePoyster of Claremont, New Hampshire, thought the exuberant combination of florals, geometrics, stripes and solids in **"Scrap Happy"** (71" x 81") precluded the need for a border. Pat simply machine-quilted it with a large meandering design and bound it with an unobtrusive print.*

## ASSEMBLY

• Cut 3 of the 16" string-pieced squares in half across the strings, as shown, to yield 6 setting triangles. Set them aside.

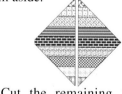

• Cut the remaining 16" string-pieced square in quarters diagonally, to yield 4 corner triangles. You will use 2. Set them aside.

• Stitch 5 diamonds together into a row, as shown. Make 3.

• Stitch 5 diamonds together into a row, as shown. Make 4.

• Referring to the quilt photo, lay out the rows. Join the rows, stopping and backstitching at the 1/4" seamline at the point of the V's.

• Set in string-pieced triangles between the rows along the short edges of the quilt. NOTE: *The triangles are oversized to allow for squaring the quilt top after assembly.*

• Stitch a corner triangle to each of the remaining corners of the quilt.

• Trim the edges of the setting and corner triangles to square the quilt.

• Finish the quilt as described in the *General Directions,* using the 2 1/2" x 44" print strips for the binding.

## Assembly Diagram

# Kerry's String Quilt

*Strategic placement of dark strips*
*adds the illusion of depth to the design.*

**QUILT SIZE:** 56" x 83"

## MATERIALS
***Choose either Option 1 or Option 2 to make this quilt.*** *(Refer to* String-Piecing Instructions.*)*

***For Option 1:***
• Assorted prints and solids, including black and other dark prints, totaling at least 7 yards
• Paper, muslin or lightweight non-fusible interfacing for the foundations

***For Option 2:***
• 8 yards of 22"-wide string-pieced fabric *(Refer to* String-Piecing Instructions.*)*
• Template plastic or freezer paper

***Also:***
• 2 1/4 yards black solid
• 5 yards backing fabric
• 60" x 87" piece of batting

## CUTTING
• Cut 14: A, black solid
• Cut 2: 3 1/2" x 78" lengthwise strips, black solid for the border
• Cut 2: 3 1/2" x 58" lengthwise strips, black solid for the border
• Cut 4: 2 1/2" x 78" lengthwise strips, black solid, for the binding

## DIRECTIONS
***Option 1:***
*Follow the* String-Piecing Instructions *to piece the foundations.*
• Trace the pattern 126 times on the foundation material, leaving a 1" space between foundations. Cut each one out 1/2" beyond the traced lines.
• Beginning at the base of a triangle foundation, stitch random width strips of assorted prints and solids to it until it is covered, as shown. NOTE: *Begin piecing at least half of the foundations with a dark or black print strip across the base of the triangle. This will create the illusion of depth in your quilt.*

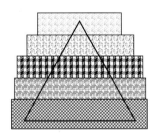

• Trim the foundation on the drawn lines. Make 126.

***Option 2:***
• Use either template plastic or freezer paper and directions in *String-Piecing Instructions* to cut 126 A's from string-pieced fabric. NOTE: *Place the base of the template(s) on a black or dark print string for at least half of the pieces. This will create the illusion of depth in your quilt.*

## ASSEMBLY
• Lay out 18 string-pieced triangles with 2 black triangles, as shown. Stitch them together to complete a vertical Row A. Make 4.

• Lay out 18 string-pieced triangles with 2 black triangles, as shown. Stitch them together to complete a vertical Row B. Make 3.
• Referring to the quilt photo as needed, lay out the vertical rows alternating A and B. Begin and end with a Row A. Join the rows.
• Trim the excess from the black triangles 1/4" beyond the outer points of the string-pieced units, as shown.

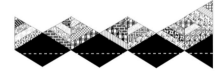

• Trim the remaining short side in the same manner.
• Measure the length of the quilt. Trim the 3 1/2" x 78" black solid strips to that measurement and stitch them to the long sides of the quilt.
• Measure the width of the quilt, including the borders. Trim the 3 1/2" x 58" black solid strips to that measurement and stitch them to the remaining sides of the quilt.
• If you used paper foundations, remove them now.
• Finish the quilt as described in the *General Directions,* using the 2 1/2" x 44" black solid strips for the binding.

*(The pattern piece for "Kerry's String Quilt" is on page 31.)*

*When Kerry left home for Kansas State University, his mother Elsie Campbell of Dodge City, Kansas, decided he needed a quilt to keep him warm. She made **"Kerry's String Quilt"** (56" x 83") with minimal effort, knowing that it would have to survive picnics, football games, band trips and 4 years of dorm living.*

# Spools

*Colorful spools of thread are the perfect inspiration for a string quilt.*

**QUILT SIZE:** 79" x 94"
**BLOCK SIZE**: 12" square

## MATERIALS
***Use Option 1 to make this quilt:***
*(Refer to* String-Piecing Instructions.*)*

• Assorted prints totaling at least 1 1/2 yards
• Assorted coordinating solids totaling at least 1 yard
• 2 yards muslin for the block backgrounds
• 3 1/2 yards white print for the sashing, border and binding
• 5 1/2 yards backing fabric
• 83" x 98" piece of batting
• Paper, muslin or lightweight non-fusible interfacing for the foundations

## CUTTING
• Cut 240: A, solid scraps in matched sets of 2, for the spool ends
• Cut 240: A, muslin, for the block backgrounds
• Cut 24: 3 1/2" x 12 1/2" strips white print, for the vertical sashings
• Cut 5: 3 1/2" x 72 1/2" lengthwise strips white print, for the horizontal sashings
• Cut 2: 3 1/2" x 83" lengthwise strips white print, for the border
• Cut 2: 3 1/2" x 98" lengthwise strips white print, for the border
• Cut 9: 2 1/2" x 44" strips white print, for the binding
• Cut 120: 4" squares, foundation material

## DIRECTIONS
*Follow the* String-Piecing Instructions *to piece the foundations.*

***For each of 30 Spools blocks:***
• Stitch random width assorted prints of a similar color to a 4" square foundation until it is covered. Make 4, using a different dominant color for each of them. Trim each foundation to 3 1/2" square.
• Lay out a string-pieced square and 2 color-coordinated matching solid A's. Position the A's so that they are parallel to the strips of string piecing. Stitch them together between the dots, as shown, backstitching at each dot, to make a spool.

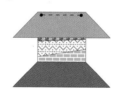

• In the same manner, stitch a muslin A to each of the remaining sides of the string-pieced square to make a spool square. Make 4.
• Fold a spool square in half diagonally, right side in. Align the unsewn edges of the two muslin A's with the two solid color A's, as shown. Stitch both seams starting, and backstitching, at the dots.

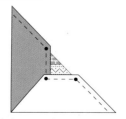

• Fold the spool square in half diagonally in the opposite direction, right side in. Align the remaining unsewn edges of two muslin A's and solid color A's. Stitch as before. Make 4.

• Arrange the four spool squares in 2 rows of 2, as shown. Sew them into rows and join the rows, to make a Spools block.

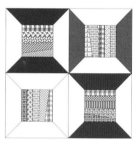

## ASSEMBLY
• Lay out 5 blocks alternately with four 3 1/2" x 12 1/2" white print sashing strips. Join them to make a block row. Make 6.
• Referring to the quilt photo, lay out the 6 block rows alternately with the 3 1/2" x 72 1/2" white print horizontal sashing strips. Join them to complete the quilt center.
• Center and stitch the 3 1/2" x 83" white print strips to the short sides of the quilt. Start, stop and backstitch 1/4" from each edge.
• Center and stitch the 3 1/2" x 98" white print strips to the remaining sides of the quilt. Start, stop and backstitch 1/4" from each edge.
• If you used paper foundations, gently remove them now.
• Miter the corners according to the *General Directions.*
• Finish the quilt as described in the *General Directions,* using the 2 1/2" x 44" white print strips for the binding.

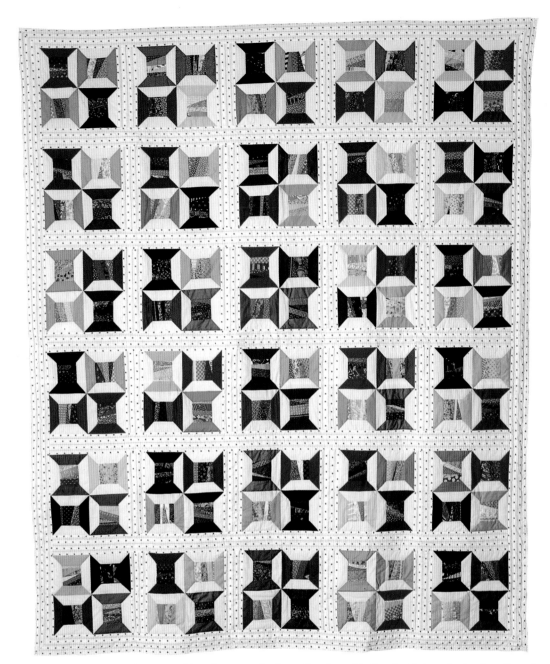

*After cutting pieces for a Tumbler charm quilt, Jean Roesler of Palisade, Colorado, had oodles of small wedge-shaped scraps left over and she couldn't bear to throw them away. This string-pieced* **"Spools"** *(79" x 94") was a great way to use them.*

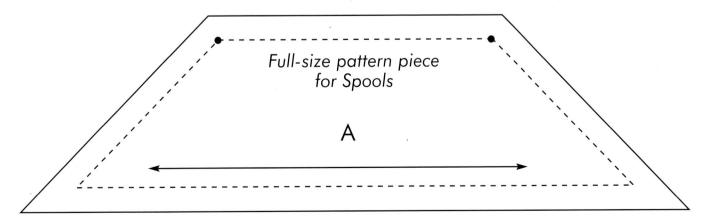

Full-size pattern piece
for Spools

A

# Kaleidoscope

*Carefully planned placement of red and orange creates a secondary design.*

**QUILT SIZE:** 65" square
**BLOCK SIZE:** 12" square

## MATERIALS
*Use Option 2 to make this quilt. (Refer to* String-Piecing Instructions.*)*

- 1/4 yard each of 25 assorted prints
- 2 yards orange
- 2 yards red
- 4 yards backing fabric
- 69" square of batting
- Template plastic
- Fabric marker

## CUTTING
- Cut 5: 1 1/2" x 32" strips, each assorted print for a total of 125 strips
- Cut 2: 4 1/2" squares, each assorted print, then cut them in half diagonally to yield 100 triangles. NOTE: *Sort them into sets of 4 of the same print.*
- Cut 4: 1 1/2" x 66" lengthwise strips, red, for the border
- Cut 5: 2 1/2" x 66" lengthwise strips, red, for the binding
- Cut 100: B, red
- Cut 4: 1 1/2" x 66" lengthwise strips, orange, for the border
- Cut 100: B, orange

## DIRECTIONS
- Make a template by tracing pattern piece A onto template plastic.
- Lay out 5 different 1 1/2" x 32" print strips. Stitch them together, along their length, to make a pieced panel. Make 25.
- Position the template on a pieced panel. With a fabric marker, trace around

the template for the first wedge. Rotate the template 1/2 turn, and mark a second wedge. Mark 2 matching sets of 4 wedges on each of the pieced panels.

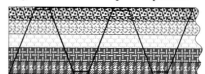

- Cut the wedges out on the marked lines. Sort them into sets of 4 identical wedges.

### For each of 25 Kaleidoscope blocks:
- Lay out 2 sets of 4 wedges, 4 orange B's, 4 red B's and one set of 4 triangles.
- Stitch a red B to the narrow end of each of 4 matching wedges, as shown, to make 4 red wedges.

- In the same manner, stitch orange B's to the narrow ends of the remaining set of wedges, to make 4 orange wedges.
- Stitch an orange wedge to a red wedge, carefully matching seams, as shown, to make a quarter-block. Make 4. NOTE: *Be sure to keep the orange wedge in the same position in each quarter block.*

- Stitch 2 quarter-blocks together to make a half-block. Make 2.

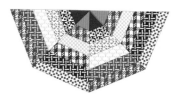

- Stitch the half-blocks together, matching center seams. Stitch matching triangles to every other wedge to complete a Kaleidoscope block.

## ASSEMBLY
- Lay out the blocks in 5 rows of 5. Stitch the blocks into rows and join the rows.
- Measure the length of the quilt. Trim two 1 1/2" x 66" red strips to that measurement. Stitch them to opposite sides of the quilt.
- Measure the width of the quilt, including the borders. Trim the remaining 1 1/2" x 66" red strips to that measurement. Stitch them to the remaining sides of the quilt.
- In the same manner, trim 2 of the

*Bright orange and red pinwheel centers add a sparkling twist to these scrappy string-pieced blocks. Patricia DePoyster of Claremont, New Hampshire, added the red and orange borders to bring an orderly finish to "**Kaleidoscope**" (65" square).*

1 1/2" x 66" orange strips to fit the quilt's length and stitch them to opposite sides of the quilt.

• Trim the remaining 1 1/2" x 66" orange strips to fit the quilt's width, and stitch them to the remaining sides of the quilt.

• Finish the quilt as described in the *General Directions*, using the 2 1/2" x 66" red strips for the binding.

*(The pattern pieces for "Kaleidoscope" are on page 30.)*

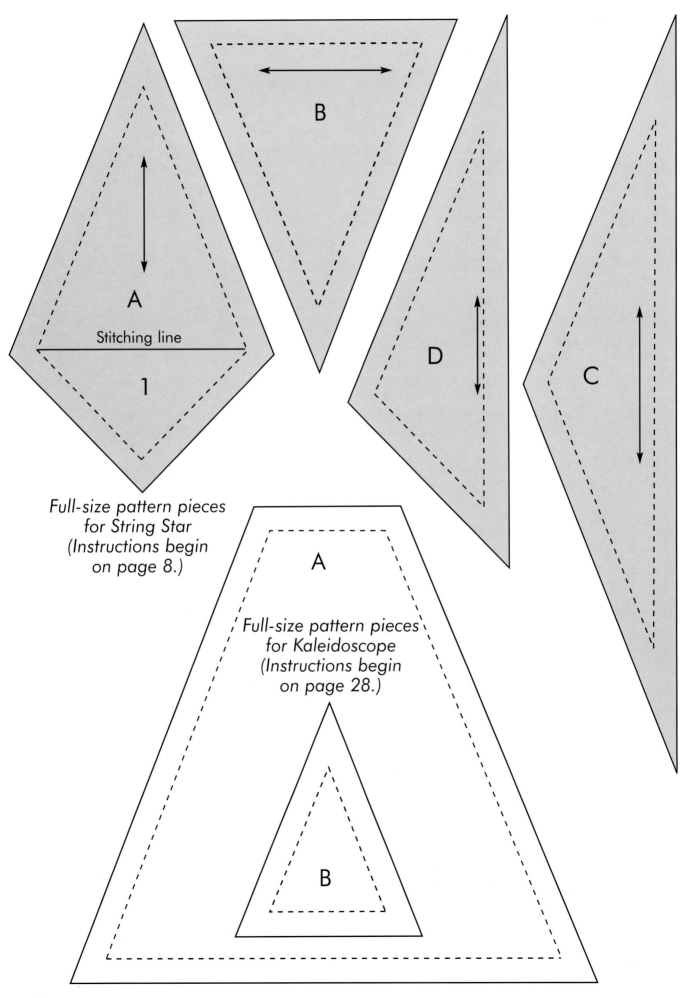

A

Stitching line

1

B

D

C

*Full-size pattern pieces
for String Star
(Instructions begin
on page 8.)*

A

*Full-size pattern pieces
for Kaleidoscope
(Instructions begin
on page 28.)*

B

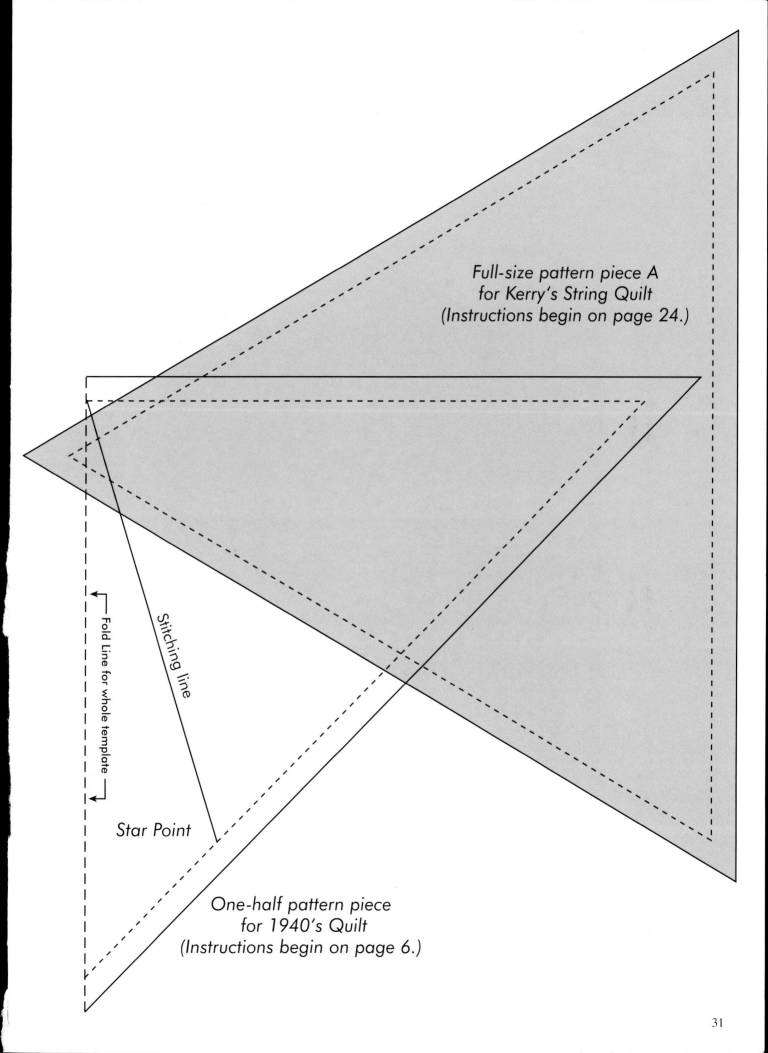

*Full-size pattern piece A*
*for Kerry's String Quilt*
*(Instructions begin on page 24.)*

Fold Line for whole template

Stitching line

*Star Point*

*One-half pattern piece*
*for 1940's Quilt*
*(Instructions begin on page 6.)*

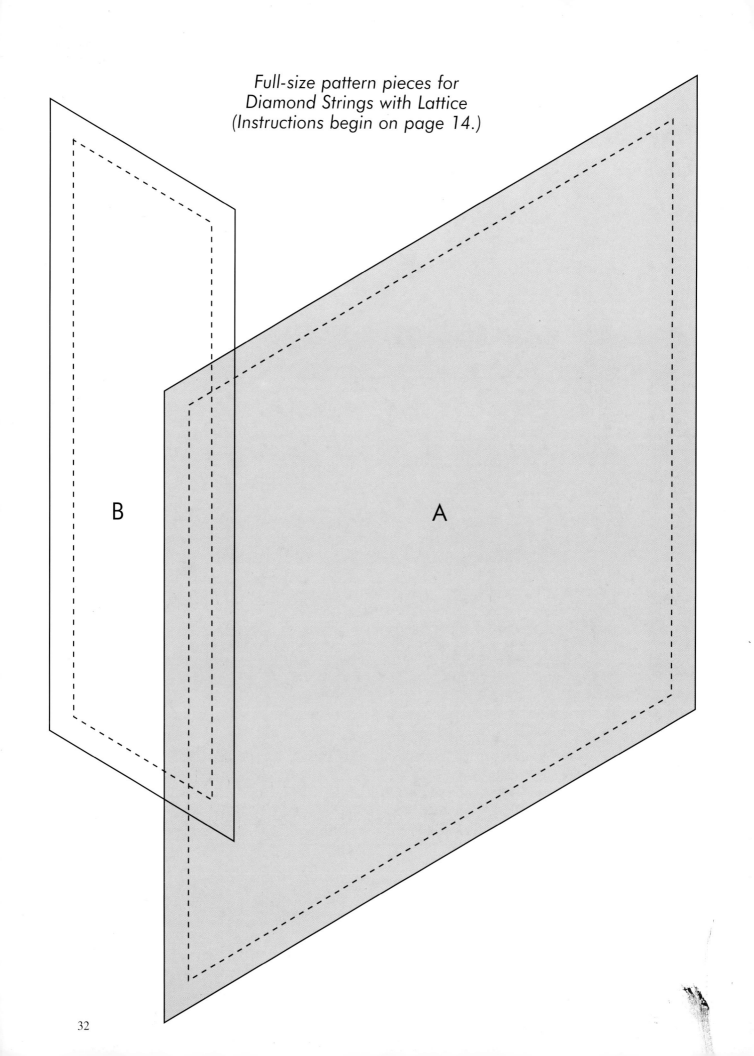

*Full-size pattern pieces for*
*Diamond Strings with Lattice*
*(Instructions begin on page 14.)*

B

A